Original title:
A Heart Full of Christmas Cheer

Copyright © 2024 Creative Arts Management OÜ
All rights reserved.

Author: Cassandra Whitaker
ISBN HARDBACK: 978-9916-94-048-8
ISBN PAPERBACK: 978-9916-94-049-5

Beneath the Boughs: Secrets of Joy

Underneath the boughs so green,
Lies a mystery, quite unseen.
With cookies missing, I must say,
Santa's diet is on display.

Elves in boots that dance and prance,
In the tinsel, they take a chance.
With jingle bells like clanging keys,
They steal the munchies, if you please.

The Promise of Peace Wrapped in Joy

A mitten lost, the cat looks shy,
While snowflakes fall, the dogs all fly.
Wrapped in laughter, we dash and skate,
The neighbors watch, they think it's fate.

Grandma's fruitcake, a hefty block,
Left on the shelf, a proper rock.
With every bite, a challenge grows,
To conquer sweets, oh, who knows woes!

Celebrations of Love, Large and Small

Lights a-twinkle, a sight so bright,
But tangled up, they spark a fight.
The tree tips over, all's askew,
Who knew the cat could steal a shoe?

In family jests and playful sighs,
With holiday glee, we roll our eyes.
Each gift unwrapped, a funny tale,
Reveals the truth: we all must fail.

Whimsical Wonders of the Festive Season

A snowman sits with carrot nose,
But why does he wear those silly clothes?
With glasses perched upon his face,
He waves and cracks jokes with such grace.

The star on top is wilting down,
While uncle dances, donning a crown.
In this season of silly cheer,
We spread our joy from ear to ear.

Echoes of Laughter in the Snow

Snowflakes dance, oh what a sight,
Kids tumble down, faces full of light.
Snowmen wobble with silly hats,
Snowball fights turn to icy spats.

In chilly air, giggles abound,
Joyful squeals echo all around.
Hot cocoa spills, marshmallows fly,
Who knew snow could make us cry?

Festive Lanterns in the Dark

Lanterns flicker with a glowing grin,
Silly reindeer dance, let the fun begin.
Candles drip, waxy mustaches grow,
Whispers of laughter in the frosty glow.

Elves skip past, their socks mismatched,
Singing carols, a tune so hatched.
One falls down, a tumble so grand,
Jingle bells ringing, isn't life splendid?

The Warm Embrace of Giving

Gifts piled high, wrapped with flair,
One's a sweater, way too rare.
Sticky fingers, bows askew,
Uncle's snoring, too much stew!

Giving socks that really don't fit,
Grandma's cookies, a sugar hit.
Laughter erupts as we unwrap,
From a crazy aunt, a fuzzy trap!

Joy Unwrapped Beneath the Tree

An avalanche of joy, gifts galore,
Dad's wild dance on the kitchen floor.
Tinsel tangled in the cat's tail,
Oh what stories we'll tell without fail!

Presents crinkle, joy all around,
Tickled pink as laughs abound.
Socks that squeak, toys that roar,
Keep this spirit forevermore!

Around the Fire, We Gathered Close

Around the fire, we roast some geeks,
Sipping hot cocoa, planning our tweaks.
Grandpa's telling tales from long ago,
We chuckle so hard, we spill on our toe!

Marshmallows fly like tiny snowballs,
Aiming at cousins, we giggle and brawl.
With laughter as warm as the flickering flame,
It's chaos and joy—oh, what a game!

Caroling Through the Whispering Pines

We stumble through pines, singing off-key,
Raccoons join in, what a sight to see!
With odd harmonies, we shake the trees,
While squirrels roll their eyes, as if to tease.

Snowflakes cling to our mismatched hats,
We belt out tunes with silly spats.
Neighbors peek out, then duck out of sight,
"Merry?" they say, "More like a fright!"

Frosted Windows, Cozy Nights

Frosted windows with stickers and glee,
We're stuck indoors, just my dog and me.
I sip my warm drink, he gives me a stare,
Wonders if I'll share, but I really don't care.

We watch the snowflakes make their ballet,
Puppy snores softly, dreaming away.
I shout, "Look! A snow angel!" he sighs,
"Just shove that guy; he's blocking my skies!"

Radiant Hearts in a Winter Wonderland

In the winter wonder, where snowmen parade,
We dance like mad under the soft, twinkling shade.
With scarves in a tangle, we trip on our feet,
Laughing at how we can't handle the heat.

The snowmen glower, their buttons askew,
As we plop down, puffed in layers, but true.
We roll like big snowballs, more fun than a dream,
In a blizzard of giggles, we melt like whipped cream!

Reverberations of Laughter

Snowmen wobble, hats askew,
Elves in chaos, that's the view.
Gingerbread men start to dance,
While cookies laugh at their sweet chance.

Santa trips on tinsel bright,
With merry giggles, pure delight.
Rudolph's nose glows red and bold,
While stories of mischief are retold.

A Quilt of Kindness and Joy

Blankets stitched with love and care,
Hot cocoa served with marshmallow flair.
Neighbors share a giggle or two,
As cheeky carolers sing askew.

Laughter wraps around the room,
As cats chase lights, pure festive gloom.
Mittens lost, but cheer remains,
Through frosty winds and joyful trains.

Treasures Found in Simple Moments

A snowball flies, oh what a fling,
A cat takes flight—what a funny thing!
Baking pies, a flour fight,
Giggles rise in pure delight.

Family jokes that make us groan,
And silly dances we've all known.
The simple joys like stars that twinkle,
Are moments stitched, not just a sprinkle.

Silent Nights of Stirring Stillness

Under blankets, stories sway,
With silly ghosts in the mix of play.
Tree lights flicker, shadows prance,
While pet dogs join in the dance.

Whispers of joy fill the air,
As socks get stuffed with love and care.
Soft giggles echo, sweet and clear,
Turning silent nights to great cheer.

A Treetop Glimpse of Magic

In the treetops, a squirrel sings,
While the cat dreams of holiday things.
Raccoons are plotting their feasts,
Under twinkling lights, they're quite the beasts.

Frosty air smells of gingerbread,
Elves dance around with sweet things in their heads.
Laughter tumbles through the snowy white,
As snowflakes giggle and take flight.

Candies and Kindness

Gumdrops and laughter fall like rain,
Candy canes make us a bit insane.
With chocolate rivers and jolly glee,
Sugar highs are the key to being free.

Peppermint marshmallows float on by,
Sipping hot cocoa, we reach for the sky.
A cookie monster steals one with a roar,
While giggles erupt from the kitchen floor.

a Sweet Exchange

Baking cookies, what a wild sight,
Flour flies like a snowy fight.
Sprinkles land like stardust dreams,
While frosting drips in sugary streams.

Gifts wrapped tight with bows so bright,
Watch them tumble, oh what a fright!
Slippers squeaking with every step,
As holiday chaos is adept.

Echoes of Laughter in the Frosty Air

Snowball fights cause slips and falls,
Laughter echoing off brick walls.
Hot cakes flipping in the pan,
Santa's belly is a brilliant plan.

Carolers croon off-key delight,
As squirrels pluck at their tiny mic flights.
With each giggle, the cold melts away,
Turning winter blues to a holiday play.

The Glow of Togetherness at Twilight

Lights twinkle as shadows dance,
Each moment a merry chance.
With socks that are mismatched by design,
We sip on cheer, a festive wine.

Under stars, the stories grow,
Of how Santa got stuck in a chimney, oh no!
With laughter bright, we hold each dear,
In each bite and chuckle, we gather cheer.

Cherished Moments Wrapped in Ribbons

Gifts piled high, oh what a sight,
Unwrapping chaos, oh what a fright!
Tangled bows and paper galore,
A cat's new toy? Oh, that's in store!

Cookies baked but burnt too dark,
Constellations of sprinkles? Let's embark!
Santa's hat upside down on my head,
Is it time for bed? No way! More bread!

Hearthside Hugs on Chilly Evenings

Warmth from the fire, socks mismatched,
Sweaters too tight, who has them patched?
With cocoa spills and marshmallows flop,
A family dance, oh what a bop!

Chasing the dog with a ho-ho-ho,
He steals the treats, but we still glow!
Chilly noses, laughter rings clear,
Who needs snow? We've got good cheer!

The Magic of Glimmering Lights

Twinkling bulbs up on the roof,
One's out? Oh no, that's the proof!
Neighbors giggle, their lights just blink,
We throw a party — don't you think?

Tinsel battles, who will win?
A ladder fall? Oh, where to begin!
Singing loudly, off-key delight,
Making memories on a chilly night!

Boughs of Evergreen and Hope

Tree scents wafting, oh what glee,
Forget the ornaments — just let it be!
A dog with a scarf, playing the fool,
We're decorating chaos, oh so cool!

With laughter spilling like hot spiced air,
An elf costume? Who? No one would dare!
Silly stories round the dinner feast,
Joyful moments that never cease!

The Spirit of Togetherness Glows

In the kitchen, cookies fly,
Flour dusting like a pie.
Grandpa's dancing, oh so spry,
While the dog just wags goodbye.

Lights are tangled, what a sight,
Twinkling, sparking, pure delight.
Singing carols off the beat,
Timmy's voice can't be discreet.

Mismatched socks upon the floor,
Mom's still searching for one more.
Laughter echoes through the hall,
As Aunt Rita takes a fall.

Family selfies, smiles abound,
Uncle's hat just fell straight down.
With every hug, our spirits soar,
We find joy in little lore.

The Beauty in Giving

Presents wrapped in paper bright,
Kids think they've got it right.
But dad's socks are the big surprise,
Gift receipts bring happy cries.

Mom's baked goods, a feast galore,
Some taste like they fell on the floor.
Cookie exchanges lead to spills,
Icing fights and sugar thrills.

A sweater from Auntie, a bit too tight,
Makes everyone giggle with all their might.
But laughter's what we really need,
In every gift, our love, we heed.

Donations from the heart begin,
Neighbors smell that turkey skin.
Every heart we reach, we cheer,
In giving, we find love so dear.

The Joy in Sharing

Gather 'round for holiday cheer,
Grumpy Grandpa's finally here.
With a joke that makes no sense,
We burst out laughing, what a fence!

Mismatched dishes at the feast,
Dinner rolls, a funny beast.
Whispers of the year's delight,
As cousins plan the next big fight.

Sharing stories, truths told bold,
Uncle Joe's tales never old.
With a wink, he steals the show,
And asserts he's the best with dough.

Hot cocoa spills and mugs run dry,
Yet joy abounds, oh me, oh my!
With each shared laugh and goofy grin,
We find the warmth that lies within.

Sweet Serenades of December

Snowflakes dance, not a care,
As I trip over my own chair.
Hot cocoa spills, oh what a sight,
Laughter echoes through the night.

The cat's in help, or so she thinks,
Paw prints everywhere, oh my, what stinks!
Carols blare from the old hi-fi,
We sing off-key, but spirits fly.

A Tapestry of Warmth and Wonder

Grandma's cookies, a sugar fest,
But guess who ate them? It's my best.
We share a glance, then burst with glee,
I'll rat you out if you rat on me!

The garland's tangled, oh what a mess,
Turns out it was a raccoon's nest!
We laugh and play, the night is bright,
In this charming holiday plight.

The Glow of Kindred Hearts

Glowing lights and silly socks,
Who needs Santa? I've got Fox.
With jingle bells and merry cheer,
We prank and laugh, oh dear, oh dear!

Eggnog spills on Auntie Sue,
She swears she'll get us back, it's true.
With giggles loud and winks so sly,
This holiday's a wacky high.

Rejoicing in the Season's Embrace

Wrapping paper flies in the fray,
"Ten bucks for this?" the kids all say.
With mischief brewing, I'll take a stand,
Next year, I swear, I'll bring the brand!

The tree leans left, we pretend it's fine,
But there's a squirrel trying to dine.
With joy and play, let the games begin,
This silly season warms us within.

Mistletoe Magic: A Season's Embrace

Underneath the leafy sprig,
We dance like fools, a little big,
You lean in close, then jump away,
My breath is minty—what a display!

Laughter echoes through the hall,
With every slip, we almost fall,
A clumsy hug and a cheeky wink,
In this festive chill, we need a drink!

Snowflakes swirl like cotton candy,
As we sway and get all dandy,
The mistletoe's a tricky friend,
It's no surprise to slip and bend!

Later, cookies stacked so high,
With frosting smiles that catch the eye,
We munch and giggle, crumbs in piles,
In this silly season, we've got our styles!

Tinsel Threads of Togetherness

The tree is bald, oh dear me!
In tinsel tangle, 'tis plain to see,
We laugh and argue—who's to blame?
The cat just pounced with stealthy fame!

Twinkling lights like stars we chase,
While wrapping gifts in frenzied race,
The paper's torn, the ribbons frayed,
Unwrap the fun, no chance of trade!

Gingerbread men in silly hats,
Do they run? Or just sit like mats?
A house of sweets, a tasty feat,
Decorated with a sticky treat!

Together we sing off-key songs,
As joy and laughter push along,
In this festive havoc we weave tight,
With friends like these, it feels just right!

Warmth in the Chill of December

Outside it's frosty, but we are bright,
In our cozy socks, oh what a sight,
The cocoa's warm, the marshmallows float,
We giggle as we watch the snow goat!

Hats too big, they flop and fall,
But in this madness, we stand tall,
Our laughter warms the coldest night,
With silly faces, we reach new heights!

Snowball fights that turn to hugs,
With frosty noses and winter shrugs,
A tumble down the icy slope,
Oh what a thrill—just hold the hope!

By the fire, we roast some cheer,
With stories told, we gather near,
Silly moments, we reminisce
In December's chill, we find our bliss!

Candles Flicker, Spirits Rise

Candles flicker, shadows play,
As we gather 'round, hip-hip-hooray,
Merry chaos fills the room,
With bundled laughter, we chase the gloom!

Stockings hung with care and fate,
We wonder if gifts are worth the wait,
A jingle bell slips from your hand,
In this mash-up, we really stand!

As cookies crumble, secrets spill,
We share our dreams with joyous thrill,
A dance-off in our living room,
Where every twirl is doubly zoom!

So raise a glass, with grins that glow,
To every silly tale we know,
Together we'll toast, let spirits soar,
In this season of cheer, we want more!

The Symphony of Us: Harmony and Cheer

In the kitchen, we dance like fools,
Whisking eggs and breaking the rules.
With flour clouds and giggling fits,
Who knew baking could come with skits?

Off-key carols fill the air,
As we squeak out tunes without a care.
The cat joins in with a meow or two,
He's the conductor, don't tell him it's true!

Our neighbors peek through the frosty glass,
Wondering what kind of chaos to amass.
With laughter echoing round the room,
We wrap our troubles in joy's bright bloom.

Every mishap becomes a treasure,
In this joyous blend of silly pleasure.
As we toast with cocoa, rich and warm,
We find delight in every charm.

Candlelight Conversations and Dreams

By candlelight, secrets we share,
Whispers of dreams, without a care.
The wax drips down with a funny plop,
While we laugh till we just can't stop.

A ghostly glare from the pumpkin pie,
As we tell tales that make us sigh.
Each slice comes with an amusing story,
Of Aunt Betty's mishaps, oh so hoary!

The lights twinkle, the shadows play,
Creating characters that dance and sway.
With marshmallows flying, we cheer and poke,
Our words weave warmth in every joke.

In this glow, we feel so free,
Every giggle a melody, a spree.
And as the night envelops our glee,
We'll share more laughs, just you and me.

Memories Played Out in Colors Bright

In a tangle of lights, we're lost for a spell,
Trying to untwist this colorful hell.
With each tangled knot, comes a burst of cheer,
As we laugh at our messy holiday sphere.

Ribbons flying like kites made of glee,
Decorating the tree with a whimsical spree.
Why hang it straight when crooked's the way?
Our masterpiece shines like a whimsical display!

Ornaments shining, some a tad shy,
Each with a tale, each with a why.
A disco ball reindeer, a jingle bell trout,
In our colorful mess, laughter's the route.

As we toast to the wildest festive spree,
With heart-shaped cookies, just you and me.
In memories cast in colors so bright,
We celebrate the joy of pure delight.

A Sprinkle of Magic in Every Cranny

Sprinkles of cheer are on every plate,
Baking mishaps that we love to state.
With gingerbread men that dance and prance,
Who knew cookies could have such a chance?

In the chaos, we find a spark,
A sprinkle of joy that lights up the dark.
With a spoon in hand, we mix and spin,
Creating a party where all can win!

The dog is wearing a holiday hat,
As we sing carols to our old cat.
We deck the halls as confetti drops,
In this magical mess, laughter never stops.

So gather around, let the good times flow,
With joy in our hearts, let silliness grow.
A sprinkle of magic in every cranny,
In this riot of fun, we're all so zany!

A Chain of Smiles and Kind Wishes

In a kitchen, cookies fly,
The cat swipes them, oh my!
Laughter erupts with each tumble,
Even the dough starts to grumble.

Wrapping gifts is quite the task,
Tape and ribbons—who needs to ask?
With each snag, we laugh and shout,
It's a wonder we don't pout!

Mismatched socks on every floor,
Who knew joy could come from a chore?
As we dance around the tree,
Even the lights start to agree.

So here's to mishaps, let's dive in,
Each giggle declared a grand win!
With smiles as bright as the star,
We celebrate near and far.

Nuances of Joy: Colors of Celebration

Red nose reindeer on the loose,
Chasing the kids—such a ruse!
Painting faces with cheer so bright,
Oops! That's not a snowball fight!

Wrapping paper goes everywhere,
A tangled mess beyond compare.
Yet amid the chaos and glee,
We share a sip of holiday tea.

Gifts that jingle, bells that clink,
Unraveling slowly, oh what a stink!
Yet every laugh lifts the air,
As we twirl without a care.

So let's paint this day with cheer,
Smile wide, hold loved ones near.
Each blunder adds a colorful touch,
These moments matter, oh so much!

Sleigh Bells Ringing, Hearts Sing

Sleigh bells jingle, quite a sound,
But watch out! The ice is profound!
Down I go with a soft thud,
But laughter follows like a flood.

Hat askew and scarf a-whirl,
Snowmen wobble as they twirl.
Did you see that dance I tried?
The snowflakes laughed, but I sighed!

With every mug of cocoa sipped,
Marshmallows jumping, quite the trip!
A sip spills here, a splash there,
Good thing that laughter's everywhere.

So let's ride this festive wave,
With smiles and tricks that we crave.
In every song, a funny note,
Together, we'll happily float!

Embracing Traditions Under the Starry Sky

Under stars, we gather round,
Traditions shared, laughter's found.
The pie we made—oh, what a sight!
Is that a hair? Nope—just a bite!

We tell the tales from years gone by,
Of uncles who always did try.
Mistakes made with every toast,
We just laugh and that's our boast!

Lights that twinkle and sometimes fail,
Yet our spirits will never pale.
When the carols start, we all sing,
Even the cat joins in for bling!

So let's raise a toast to fun and cheer,
To those we love, who hold us dear.
In every moment, a joyful blend,
At the end of the day, it's all pretend!

The Spirit of Giving Glows Bright

In a time of joy and delight,
We share our snacks, quite a sight.
A fruitcake tossed from the tall shelf,
Lands with a thud, all by itself.

Wrapping paper scattered about,
As family laughs and shouts,
Gift cards missed the proper route,
A sock for me? I want a pout!

The reindeer's antlers are too small,
Like no one saw the mighty fall.
With tinsel tangled in my hair,
I dance like I just don't care.

So let's raise a toast with cold tea,
To every kind of gift that's free!
A season bright, a quirky blend,
With laughter loud that never ends.

Love Wrapped in Red and Green

Wrap it up in satin bows,
A sweater, two sizes above, I suppose.
Colored lights blink on and off,
While Uncle Joe has a coughing scoff.

The cookies are burnt, or so they claim,
But Grandma insists they taste the same.
With sprinkles flying like confetti,
The dog snags one—he's mighty Betty!

A gift exchange gone hilariously wrong,
The singing is loud, and off-key along.
Tangled cords and crumbling tags,
Someone's got to dodge the lags!

So gather 'round with cheer and fun,
Embrace the chaos, everyone!
For love wrapped tight is all we need,
Even if it's just a bag of seed.

Baking Cookies and Making Memories

Flour flies as we bake with glee,
Sticky fingers, oh, woe is me!
Measuring cups spill all around,
Our laughter echoes; what a sound!

A gingerbread man lost his way,
I blame the dog—so what can I say?
Icing missed, and cookies burn,
Who thought this would be our year to learn?

Rolling dough like a tumbling fool,
Splattered frosting, what a rule!
Little hands make the biggest mess,
But with each giggle, we're truly blessed.

With sugar highs and goofy grins,
We dance like loons, not afraid to spin.
So here's to fun and sweet delights,
Making memories on frosty nights.

Snowflakes Dance in Eager Hearts

Outside it flurries, we're bundled tight,
  Snowflakes swirl, a snowy delight.
  Tommy's snowman is quite the sight,
With a carrot nose that's wobbled right.

  We race on sleds down icy hills,
In our quest for laughter and silly thrills.
  Hot cocoa spills — oh what a gleam,
A marshmallow floating, what a dream!

  Snowball fights and laughter loud,
  We're the happiest, snowy crowd.
  Slipping and sliding, we try to flee,
But laughter's winter's best decree!

So as the flakes dance without care,
We embrace the chill with joy to share.
Let's make a moment, soak in the fun,
  Until all the laughter comes undone.

Starlit Wishes and Dreams Unfurled

In the dark, a twinkle glows,
The neighbors dance in funny clothes.
Cookies burned, a smoky plight,
Yet their laughter fills the night.

Snowflakes fall like cotton balls,
Kids are sliding down the halls.
A dog steals all the treats galore,
Racing 'round, barking for more!

Chasing red-nosed reindeer dreams,
While dad's dressed in sparkly themes.
Jingle bells now out of whack,
As grandma tries to find her snack.

So raise a cup with frothy cheer,
To funny times that bring us near.
In this season, laughter's real,
Let's cherish each ho-ho-ho appeal.

Laughter's Echo in the Frosty Air

Frosty noses, hat askew,
Snowball fights, oh what a view!
Belly laughs and silly falls,
Echo through the frozen halls.

A snowman teeters, starts to sway,
When cousin Jim hops in the fray.
With carrots stuck, it starts to frown,
As laughter bubbles all around.

Candy canes stuck in the door,
While baking leads to flour war.
"It's all in good fun!" cries Aunt Claire,
With icing smeared across her hair.

So sing and dance in winter's light,
With funny tales to share tonight.
For in this joy, we'll always find,
The laughter left with love entwined.

The Scent of Pine and Joyful Kiss

Pine-scented hugs and cookie bliss,
Under mistletoe we sneak a kiss.
Uncle Joe's dancing with the cat,
While Aunt Sue giggles, "Imagine that!"

Wrapping gifts with tape amiss,
Even Dad may need a kiss.
His bright red sweater, oh so free,
Got stuck on the lamp, what a sight to see!

Lights that twinkle, flicker bright,
Cousins tangled in string's delight.
A wreath that fell with such a clatter,
We laugh so hard, we just might splatter!

In this chaos, love's the spark,
With every cheer, we light the dark.
For every giggle and every grin,
The joy of this season draws us in.

Gathered Around the Hearth of Love

Gather 'round the crackling fire,
With hot cocoa, we all conspire.
Stories told with playful glee,
As dad insists he's as cool as can be.

With marshmallows flying high,
And Grandma yelling, "Oh, don't try!"
The flames flicker, shadows dance,
In this joyful, funny circumstance.

Sweaters worn two sizes too big,
While cousin Mike does a silly jig.
Pet dog snoozing near the heat,
Dreaming of cookies, oh what a treat!

So raise a cheer for all to see,
For each funny moment, wild and free.
In this evening filled with joy,
Let's hold each other, girl and boy.

Cinnamon and Snowflakes in the Air

The cookies are burning, oh what a feat,
The dog snatched a pie, now he's quite the treat!
Snowflakes are falling, right onto my nose,
I tripped on a wreath, now everyone knows!

Deck the halls with laughter, the garland's a mess,
Grandma's got tinsel caught in her dress.
The lights are all twinkling, but only one stays,
Each time we plug in, the circuit dismays!

Our tree leans to the left, it's quite a sight!
I swear it's just tired from last Christmas night.
With each squeaky ornament, we all take a cheer,
For every mishap, we just pour another beer!

With ribbons and bows wrapped 'round Auntie Sue,
She says "I was trying," we all just knew.
This season's a circus, we wouldn't want less,
Gather round for the fun, and forget all the stress!

Radiance of Yuletide Blessings

The lights on my house blink like a dance,
The neighbors are staring, is this a romance?
We sing out of tune and our dog runs away,
He thinks it's a howling, so why won't he stay?

Uncle Joe dressed as Santa gives us a fright,
With a belly-full pie spilling out in the night.
He slipped on some ice, fell straight on his back,
Yelled "Ho ho ho!" as he went for the snack!

The stockings are hung in a lopsided row,
Filled with odd trinkets, like socks of a show.
A cat in a reindeer hat prances around,
Tugging the ribbons that once were so sound!

As carolers gather, we join the parade,
We laugh at our rhymes, oh what a charade!
With smiles all around, this season's bright cheer,
We'll revel in joy, despite holiday fear!

Carols in the Candlelight

Candlelight flickers as we sing off-key,
It's hard not to laugh when we all can't agree.
Ghosts of the past join our festive delight,
Grandpa's old stories make everyone bright.

The choir is missing, was someone on blast?
The cats are now hiding, this cheer won't last.
Jingle bells jangle with a thrilling ring,
While Auntie's surprise dance is a dubious thing!

Potatoes are mashed but the gravy's just soup,
With laughter and love, we all join the troop.
Gather round family, this circus of cheer,
With each funny moment, our spirits grow near!

So raise up a glass to this night we embrace,
To funny old memories, and a warm, cozy space.
The candles may drip, but we won't mind a bit,
For this is the season where giggles are lit!

Spirit of Togetherness Under the Mistletoe

Under the mistletoe, we all make a dash,
Old Uncle Bob kissed the cat, oh what a clash!
With giggles around, we all take the chance,
The Christmas tree toppled—such an odd dance!

Timmy's new sweater has glitter galore,
He's looking like Rudolph with bling we adore.
Each gift's a surprise, wrapped up with a grin,
A tea set for Dad, and he'll never win!

As we gather 'round, with hot cocoa in tow,
The marshmallows float, like the dreams of the snow.
We swap all our stories, the smiles fill the room,
Who cares about carols when we're dancing with gloom?

So here's to the laughter, the jokes that we share,
The spirit of joy, it fills up the air.
With every sweet mishap, we cherish the night,
Together in chaos, we're bursting with light!

Starlit Memories of Joyful Gatherings

Under twinkling lights, we dance with glee,
Laughter echoes wide, like a jolly spree.
Grandma's fruitcake wobbles, a sight to behold,
We run from the table, so brave and so bold.

Presents fly open, confetti in the air,
A pair of odd socks for cousin Claire.
With every loud giggle and silly little bling,
Joy bounces around, oh, what fun we bring!

Outside there's a snowman, with a smile so wide,
His carrot nose droops, but he takes it in stride.
We sing to the moon, in our mismatched shoes,
Who knew the stars loved our holiday blues?

So here's to the moments, both silly and bright,
In our cozy old living room, laughter takes flight.
With cookies and cocoa, we toast to the fun,
These starlit memories sparkle, our hearts quickly spun.

Love's Letters Adorned with Glitter

Scribbles on stationery, jealousy thrives,
A love note from Grandma, but who really survives?
With glitter all over, the cat gets a bath,
And Uncle Joe's coffee makes quite the mad math!

In envelopes crinkled, mail's all askew,
Dear Aunt Edna's checks, with a stamp or two.
We gather around, to read with delight,
What's in the next letter? Oh, what a sight!

With wish lists and dreams, they fly with a grin,
But our dog steals the post—let the fun begin!
We chase him in circles, through wreaths of bright red,
Love's letters in chaos, but joy is widespread.

So here's to the laughter, with each silly word,
In the flurry of cheer, let no spirit be stirred.
When love's in the air, and glitter's amiss,
These letters remind us, that joy is pure bliss.

Whimsical Delights of Merry Hearts

Oh, joy in the kitchen, where cookies collide,
Flour on noses, and crumbs we can't hide.
The dog snatches snacks, runs like a pro,
While we trip on the carpet—oh, what a show!

Mismatched ornaments hang on the tree,
Each telling a story, just for you and me.
Grandpa's old hat is now on the cat,
They twirl like a ballerina, how about that?

On sleds we go crashing, the hill's quite a ride,
The snowball fights raging, with snowflakes as pride.
With giggles and shouts, we breathe in the cheer,
These whimsical moments bring us ever near.

So dance in the chaos, let mischief take flight,
With laughter and joy, we shout through the night.
Under twinkling stars, let all troubles depart,
In this season of whimsy, we warm every heart.

Evergreen Whispers of Joy

The scent of the pine makes us laugh and cheer,
Each needle a whisper, "The season is here!"
With elves in the attic and reindeer afloat,
Where socks disappear, like a clever magician's coat.

On the roof there's a ruckus, what could it be?
A raccoon in a Santa hat climbs our old tree.
We gather to watch, as our patience goes thin,
With candy cane battles, and giggles begin.

Sipping hot cocoa, each sip's a delight,
But the marshmallows hop, like they're destined for flight.
A toast to the madness, the joys that ensue,
In the evergreen magic, we laugh, me and you.

So gather around, let the stories unfold,
With mischief and laughter, each moment we hold.
In this moment of joy, let the fun never stop,
Through evergreen whispers, our happiness hops.

Joyful Whispers of Winter Nights

Snowflakes dance in comical flight,
A squirrel in a hat, what a sight!
Laughter bounces from chimney to roof,
As we roast marshmallows, it's all goof!

Hot cocoa spills with a frothy cheer,
The cat's in a sweater, oh dear, oh dear!
Just when you think it can't get worse,
The dog steals a cookie, oh, what a curse!

Twinkling lights hang at odd angles,
While Grandma tries out her jingle dangles.
The kids throw snow at the neighbor's dog,
And he returns it, wrapped in a fog!

As carols echo through snowy lanes,
This silliness surely serves as gains.
Joy spreads wide like the Christmas lights,
On this winter night of merry delights!

Tinsel Dreams and Frosted Wishes

Tinsel shimmers with a cheeky grin,
As cats want to dive in like a win!
We hang lights while we trip on the floor,
Oops! There goes Grandpa, right out the door!

Cookies set out with a hopeful vibe,
But who knew the kids make them with bribe?
Elf hats on dogs, tethered with glee,
They're plotting to eat all the sweets, just wait and see.

Snowmen wobble in laughter so loud,
With carrot noses, they make us proud!
The children giggle at their own hair,
The jigs and jags that dance in the air!

As the night fills with whispering grins,
Holiday fun, where absurdity wins.
Frosted wishes float on each breath,
In this season's play, we dance with zest!

The Sparkle of Kindness

Neighbors share pies, though they did burn,
The dog snags a slice—oh, have we learned!
Presents wrapped in tape and all stuck,
Looks like Santa's had a bit of bad luck!

Ribbons tangled in a messy mess,
As kids sing loud, oh what a stress!
The tree lights flicker, but who really cares?
Beneath the chaos, kindness flares.

Snowball fights pull pants down with glee,
While hot cider spills just like tea.
Look at those mittens, such mismatched flair,
Who knew fashion could cause such despair?

With laughter that bubbles both light and bright,
We gather together, holding each tight.
In this whimsical dance of warmth and cheer,
The sparkle of kindness is always near!

Mirth in the Starlit Silence

Midnight news of a snowman fight,
With carrots flying, what a sight!
Sleigh bells jingle, the raccoons are near,
Sipping from cocoa cups, oh dear, oh dear!

Under the stars, bright lights do twinkle,
Grandpa's high notes give us a crinkle.
Silly jokes fill the frosty air,
As smelly socks slip from the chair!

A dance-off ensues by the Christmas tree,
With moves so goofy, how can it be?
We sway and laugh, the world spins around,
In this starlit silence, joy can be found.

As laughter echoes through glimmering night,
Friendship wraps us, oh what a delight!
This season brings whimsy, a riotous cheer,
In our cozy circles, we hold loved ones near!

Cocoa Dreams by the Fireside

Sipping cocoa, sweet and warm,
My cat plots a festive charm.
Marshmallows float with glee,
While I dodge the dog's big sneeze.

The fireplace crackles bright,
As embers dance away the night.
Grandma's hat's a little tight,
Her wig's a flying kite in flight!

Outside, the snowflakes wear a grin,
As I trudge through drifts, my socks are thin.
With every slip, I let out a howl,
My friends just laugh, they love to scowl!

So here we toast with mugs in hand,
In a nutty, warm and joyful land.
Let cocoa dreams make spirits soar,
With laughter ringing through the door.

The Dance of Frosty Joy

Frosty prances in the street,
With candy canes tucked in his seat.
He trips on lights, oh what a sight,
Then does a jig that feels so right!

The neighbors cheer and join the show,
While snowmen wobble, keeping low.
A twirl, a spin, a snowy fling,
Frosty sings and starts to swing!

A squirrel steals a shiny ball,
While kids slip, they giggle, then fall.
Hot chocolate spills; oh, what a mess!
But laughter sparkles, we feel so blessed!

So gather 'round for fun and cheer,
As Frosty's dance brings us near.
In snowball fights and chilly glee,
It's pure delight—we're wild and free!

Embracing the Light Within

Twinkling lights on every tree,
But wait, is that a raccoon I see?
It's pilfering tinsel with such grace,
Turning my yard into a sparkly place!

Friends gather round for a holiday feast,
While Uncle Joe wears a turkey beast.
With silly jokes that make us howl,
We joke he's lost his festive prowl!

The warmth of laughter fills the air,
With faux pas galore, no need to care.
In this glow, we find our glow,
A jumble of joy, all in a row.

So let's embrace each silly cheer,
As wild memories draw us near.
With hearts aglow, we'll always be,
A quirky crew, wild and free!

Festooned Allure of Wonder

With garlands hung and bells that jingle,
My dog chases shadows, starts to mingle.
Whiskers twitch as he leaps and bounds,
With every crash, his charm resounds!

Cookies crumble, the cat takes a bite,
Leaves me longing for more tonight.
Though sprinkles scatter! What a sight,
My baking failure shines so bright!

We cheer on games that go awry,
As Aunt Sue winds up getting spry.
Her dance moves? Oh dear, they're quite bizarre,
Yet we clap for her—that's our star!

So here's to laughter, joy, and cheer,
With quips and antics—bring them near!
In this festival of playful blunder,
We find our peace, our festooned wonder!

The Gifts We Give and Receive

Wrapped in paper, oh so neat,
Dancing socks find happy feet.
A toaster sings, a cat's delay,
Unwanted gifts can save the day.

Shiny boxes stacked up high,
A rubber chicken makes us sigh.
A mystery box sparks great debate,
With laughter loud, we can't be late.

Symphony of Laughter and Lights

Twinkling lights that blink and dance,
Chaotic tunes make folks prance.
Mismatched socks, and silly hats,
Our neighbors think we're all just bats.

Bells that jingle, giggles fly,
As nutcrackers teach us to try.
With cocoa spills and cookie fights,
Our home's a show of pure delights.

Evergreen Memories

Pine needles stuck in every nook,
A dog steals treats, a classic look.
Ornaments hang on every sill,
Grandma's secret stash gives us a thrill.

The tree leans left, it seems to snooze,
Mom yells, 'That's not how you choose!'
We laugh at moments, fun in the air,
With memories woven beyond compare.

Timeless Love

His gift wraps me in a cozy hug,
But socks, no thanks, I feel a tug.
She laughs with glee at my old ties,
We trade our quirks, what a surprise!

Dinner's a dance, what could go wrong?
Burned the turkey, but still sing our song.
Through chaotic cheer and holiday spin,
We share a wink, where love begins.

Starry Nights and Sugarplum Delights

With candy canes and puppies galore,
We're wrapped in joy from ceiling to floor.
Pajamas mismatched, the kids run wild,
While visions of sweets make us all smiled.

Gingerbread men, the icing's a mess,
In our holiday chaos, we must confess.
With fairy tales and silly fright,
We laugh together under the starlight.

Threads of Unity in a Chaotic World

In a world where chaos reigns, we find,
Laughter threads us close, no need to unwind.
Jingle bells and tangled lights,
Bring joy as we bicker through festive nights.

Grandma's cookies, a holiday test,
Sprinkled flour makes a cozy mess.
While sugar plums dance in dreams so sweet,
We trip over gifts, laughing at our feet.

Neighbors squabble over lawn displays,
Reindeer on rooftops cause wild delays.
Yet through all quirks, we share the mirth,
In our merry mayhem, we find our worth.

We gather 'round to toast with cheer,
Grumbling about the holiday beer.
Each silly squabble, a thread divine,
Stitching hearts together, oh so fine.

Yuletide Reflections and Heartfelt Connections

Under the mistletoe, we stand aloof,
Pouty faces where love is the proof.
Wrapped up in layers, we try to fit,
Fumbling with kisses, how silly we sit.

Tinsel flies and the tree leans low,
Dad's again stuck in the lights' mad show.
The cat's in the branches, what a grand sight,
As we giggle and dodge falling pine tonight.

Eggnog flowing but the jokes won't cease,
A toast to the awkward, may they find peace.
Each family story, both silly and bold,
Crafts a warm quilt in the wintery cold.

Through laughter and chaos, we find our way,
These hilarious blunders make bright our day.
For in these reflections, we all come to see,
The joy in connections, both wild and free.

Dances with Shadows and Candles Glow

As shadows dance in the candlelight,
We giggle at secrets we can't hold tight.
Snowflakes twirl in the frosty air,
While we prance around with a festive flair.

The Christmas ham gives its best pose,
While Auntie claims she'll never disclose.
Cooking misadventures that bring a cheer,
"Did anyone order fruitcake this year?"

Kids dreaming loud as they snore in bliss,
While grown-ups whip up a cheerful hiss.
The tree's glowing, but oh what a fight,
To keep the decorations straight and right.

Each flicker of light brings a chuckle near,
In this dance of shadows, there's nothing to fear.
For laughter's the song, and we're all in tow,
In the warmth of the season, we happily glow.

A Tapestry of Light in the Dark

In the tapestry woven with laughter so bright,
We cling to each other through the chilly night.
Boughs of holly and twinkling stars,
Our silly antics stitch love into scars.

The sweater you wore is a fashion faux pas,
Yet it brings a giggle, oh well, ha ha!
Singing carols, unsure of the tune,
Under snowflakes falling, we make quite the swoon.

Mismatched socks peek from under the tree,
Each gift wrapped with care, won't you wait and see?
With whispers and giggles, we pass quite the note,
The surprise of your life in a fancy old coat.

As we gather 'round, the chaos is clear,
But joy fills the room, it's all that we hear.
So here's to the holidays, the laughter, the bliss,
In this tapestry of light, it's you I won't miss.

Festive Echoes in Every Corner

The stockings are hung, but one fell down, A reindeer's been sighted, just over the town. My cat's in a lamp, with a look of surprise, As I juggle the cookies, they start to fly!

The lights are all flashing, it's quite a display, But last year's old tinsel won't go away. I trip on the garland, a scene for the show, As laughter erupts, the eggnog starts to flow.

Uncle Joe's holiday dance is a sight, He spins with the turkey, what a strange flight! Cousins in pajamas, they all start to cheer, While Dad's stuck singing his "favorite" song here.

So here's to the chaos, the joy that it brings, The sprightly fun chaos of silly old things. With giggles and cheer, we all will partake, In the messiest Christmas, make no mistake!

The Dance of Joy: A Celebration of Life

In the kitchen, there's sugar, a sprinkle of glee, Aunt Betty's lost count of her cookies, you see. She's dancing with flour, what a wild sight, A twirl, a plop, then a cookies' delight!

The tree's getting taller, but it's not straight, The ornaments wobble; it's a comical fate. As the dog tries to jump, and the cat runs away, I swear it's a circus, come join in the play!

Grandma's on bingo, shouting with flair, But while we all focus, she's winning the chair! The party is lively, the punch isn't spiked, Just watch for the floor; someone's about to slide.

It's laughter, it's friendship, it's moments we save, In this festive celebration, we all misbehave. So raise up your drinks, let's toast to the night, For joy is the dance and we're feeling it right!

Warm Glow of Friendship by the Fire

By the fire, we gather, the marshmallows roast, Bob's face is all blackened; he's eating the most. We share all our stories, amusing and bright, Greg claims he saw Santa; that's quite the delight!

The cocoa's too hot; it spills on my shoe, My friend laughs so hard, there's hot chocolate, too. We wear those ugly sweaters with pride, Only to find out, they shrank in the tide.

Laughter erupts, as songs fill the space, But Dave hits the high note, it's quite out of place. The dog joins the chorus, howls every tune, While we end up dancing under the moon.

Here's to good friends, and their wonderful cheer, This firelight gathering feels perfect and dear. We roast silly wishes, together we climb, For these moments, my friend, are the laughter of time!

Songs of the Season Beneath the Moon

Under the stars, we gather and sing, With twinkling lights wrapped in everything. Old Doug's got a kazoo, it's painfully loud, But we dance and we laugh, we're a festive crowd!

The weather is chilly, but warm is the cheer, When Martha drops cookies, and chugs down her beer. She's claiming the title of Christmas champ, But splattered with icing, we laugh at her lamp!

The snowflakes keep falling, it's turning to slush, Little kids are sledding, they make quite the rush. While parents are standing, just watching the sight, We share all the giggles that fill up the night.

So raise up your voices, let spirits arise, Beneath all the twinkling, let laughter be the prize. For songs of the season bring joy like no other, With friends all around—what could be better?

Cherishing Each Moment as It Flies

Snowmen wear hats way too big,
Jingle bells sound like a pig.
Cookies vanish with a cheer,
Elves sneak in for a pint of beer.

Holiday lights are taped to the floor,
Cat climbs up, but can't take more.
The tree leans like it's had some gin,
Each glance at it makes us grin.

Grandma's fruitcake's a funny sight,
It bounces like it's ready to fight.
Joyful chaos, laughter in the air,
Mom says, 'Next year, I swear, I'll prepare!'

From snowball fights to hot cocoa,
Each moment's wild—a real show.
We'll cherish these, as time flies,
With giggles and silly, surprised eyes.

Embracing the Magic

Nose so red like Rudolph's nose,
We dance like we're wiggly worms in clothes.
Santa's list is full of tricks,
Who knew he loved magic flicks?

Chimney smoke and cookies on the roof,
Reindeers jump, give us a woof.
Mistletoe hangs, it's time to kiss,
Uncle Fred just aims for the cheese bliss.

The holiday cards all face the wall,
Granny's pajamas? The best of them all!
With laughter and toys piled high,
We embrace this magic, oh my!

Neighbors shout with spirit so bright,
Whoever thought 'twould take flight?
Each hug feels warm and slightly weird,
In this joyful time—don't be steered!

Holding it Tight

Hot cocoa spills on Dad's new chair,
Laughter echoes—oh, what a scare!
We hold our joy, that spirit bites,
As we pull on sweaters that surely fright.

Someone's got glitter stuck on their nose,
Every gesture a clumsy pose.
Holding onto hugs that are wide,
In this funny dance, now let's glide!

Grandpa swears he'll cook the turkey,
We think he just might end up murky.
Family antics, toss 'em high,
A holiday feast; who'll try to fly?

So raise a glass—what a sight,
Cheers to the times we hold tight!
In all the mess and cheery spree,
We laugh together, you and me.

Lights in the Window: Hope in the Heart

Lights twinkle like they're having fun,
Flickering wildly; oh, what a run!
We sing carols slightly off-key,
Our neighbors just smile, they're all so free.

Cookies crumbled all over the floor,
Sweetened laughter—they beg for more.
Our hopes glow bright, like stars in the sky,
With giggles and facts that make us fly.

In the window, a snowman looks cold,
But our hearts stay warm, young and old.
Each Clark Griswold moment we share,
Is a dance of spirit, funny and rare!

So raise those lights, let 'em beam,
Spread that joy, and chase the dream.
With every chuckle, our spirits ignite,
As hope in our hearts shines so bright.

Serenity in the Dance of Snowflakes

Snowflakes fall with a swoosh and a spin,
Landing on noses with a cheeky grin.
Joyously dancing from the sky,
Beware of snowballs—oh my!

Each flurry flinks through the air,
Catching a ride on the dog's soft hair.
We glide together, right on down,
Lazy laughter—who wears the crown?

The world turns soft with a blanket white,
Hot cider spills—it's a wonderful sight!
With each little twirl of frosty delight,
We stumble and giggle, oh what a night!

So let's dance with snowflakes in the air,
With friends and family, no room for despair.
Embracing the joy, oh what a flight,
In the magic of winter, everything's right!

The Warmth of Hands Held Tight

In mittens we struggle, fingers entwined,
Hot cocoa spills, leaving marshmallows behind.
We laugh as we trip, over tinsel and strings,
While caroling cats join in, oh the joy they bring!

A snowman awaits, his eyes gleam with glee,
His carrot nose winks, says, "Come play with me!"
With snowballs in hand, we step back in time,
And giggles erupt in this winter's rhyme.

Hot chocolate mustache, we sip with delight,
A peppermint twist makes everything right.
As snowflakes dance down, like confetti in air,
We cherish these moments, none can compare!

So here's to the warmth, all wrapped up in cheer,
With laughter and joy, we hold each one near.
In the chill of the night, our spirits take flight,
Together we cherish this magical night!

Glimmers of Hope in Winter's Grasp

Outside, it's a wonderland, quite a display,
Inside it's a circus, with games in the fray.
Grandpa's wearing reindeer horns, quite absurd,
And Aunt Sally's dancing like a silly bird!

The tree's decorations are wobbly at best,
With popcorn and glitter, we surely jest.
While cookies we bake turn out slightly charred,
We eat them with laughter, we're quite unscarred!

The fire crackles loudly, a playful roar,
While we tell wild stories that we can't ignore.
Oh, the tales of the elves and their mischievous deed,
Bring joy to our hearts, it's all that we need!

In winter's strong grip, we find little joys,
Laughter erupts, big smiles from the boys.
So, join us tonight, the fun will amass,
With winks and giggles, time sure flies fast!

Hearts Aglow: A Tapestry of Cheer

Our socks mismatched, we giggle away,
As the dog steals the gifts, oh what a play!
With a sleigh full of fun, we dash down the hall,
Who knew winter blues could be so enthralled?

The garland's now tangled, it captures the light,
A jingle bell chorus welcomes the night.
As we stamp our feet, and warm up our toes,
With each little twinkle, our laughter just grows.

A knock at the door, who's there but a friend?
With cookies in hand, let the fun never end!
We raise our hot drinks, a toast to the chill,
Let every warm moment linger, until.

Mirth fills the air, like snowflakes that fall,
Together we're happy, in this grand brawl.
Wrap up in warmth, let the good times ensue,
For in this merry chaos, there's joy in the brew!

Lights that Sparkle, Eyes that Shine

The twinkling lights dance like fireflies bright,
While Grandma wraps up, snug in her woolly sight.
We chase down the cat, in a game of delight,
Who knew holiday spirit could start quite the fight?

With grandpa's old stories, our cheeks start to ache,
As he teases the kids about chocolate cake.
While Uncle Joe hums a tune, off-key,
It's a concert of joy, just let laughter be free!

With mittens and scarves, we venture outside,
Building snow forts, in the cold we will bide.
As snowballs fly, our spirits ignite,
It feels like the world is just filled with delight!

So let's toast to the season, with a wink and a cheer,
The warmth of the moment, forever held dear.
In the glow of the lights, our happiness shines,
Through laughter and joy, our love intertwines!

Sipping Cocoa under Starry Veils

Under the stars, we sip hot brew,
Marshmallows floating, like dreams come true.
Fingers turn pink from mugs held tight,
We laugh at the squirrels in their silly flight.

The cat sits bold, eyeing all the guff,
While snowflakes dance, it's holiday stuff.
We're wrapped in blankets, cozy and round,
Wishing for cookies that never came down!

The snowman grins, his carrot quite sly,
Waving to cars as they scoot by.
With cocoa drips on our cheerful clothes,
We giggle anew at the festive flows.

Outside it's chilly, inside it's bright,
The laughter flickers like twinkling lights.
We take one more sip, with a wink and a cheer,
Celebrating this season, from far and near.

Cherished Moments: A Woven Tale

In the warmth of the room, we gather and grin,
Hoping Auntie won't serve her fruit cake again.
Baking cookies while wearing our hats,
Can't find the flour, just crumbs from the cats!

We hang silly socks, mismatched and loud,
Expecting presents to please the whole crowd.
Uncle Joe's snoring, the dog's on the floor,
We take turns cringing, behind the closed door.

The lights twinkle bright, like stars gone amiss,
While we all join in for a group Christmas kiss.
Don't tell Grandma, or she'll bake us a pie,
Too many calories, oh my, oh my!

In moments like these, our laughter is grand,
With memories woven like grains in the sand.
Each funny tale adds to joy that we share,
In the tapestry woven of love and good care.

The Dance of Snowflakes and Wishes

Snowflakes are swirling, a wild little dance,
While kids in the street take a chance to prance.
With snowballs a-flying, they all seem so spry,
Until one hits Dad and he lets out a sigh!

The trees wear their coats, all sparkly and white,
While we slip and slide, oh what a sight.
Mom's on the porch, with a laugh and a shout,
Just made a snow angel, what's that all about?

Wishes fly up like the stars in the night,
As we all share secrets with pure delight.
A snowman pops up, grin wide and full,
"Hey, is it winter or just ridiculous cool?"

As ducks on a pond, we wiggle and gleam,
In the magic of winter, we dance and we dream.
With hops and with skips and some silly falls,
We cherish this season, in laughter it calls.

Gifts from the Heart: Unseen Treasures

Presents wrapped bright, some shine, some flop,
We guess through the paper, we're hoping to stop.
A box shaped like fish, oh what can it be?
Is Grandpa still pranking us? Just wait and see.

The tree leans a bit, a new ornament waits,
Made by the kids, from a box of old plates.
We smile and we ooh, as they hang it just right,
"I think it looks great—oh, what a fun sight!"

Our laughter's the best gift, it can't be disguised,
Like wrapping up love, it's truly surprise!
With games and with giggles, we cherish the fun,
Celebrating moments that make us feel young.

So here's to the stories, the songs that we share,
To gifts from the heart, they're beyond compare.
With joy in the air, and light in our eyes,
We welcome the season, with sweet, funny sighs.

Milton Keynes UK
Ingram Content Group UK Ltd.
UKHW021240191124
451300UK00007B/166